Ice Crystal Robbery

by Chris Parker
Illustrated by Bill Ledger

OXFORD

UNIVERSITY PRESS

In this story ...

Jin
(Swoop)

Jin has the power to fly. He can go as high as a rocket!

Miss Linen
(teacher)

Ben
(Sprint)

Slink
(Combat Cat)

Miss Linen was showing the class a new cape.
It was designed to protect them from the cold.
"Can I have a volunteer please?" Miss Linen said.

Jin put his hand up. "Pick me!"
Miss Linen handed Jin the cape. Then she picked up a jar of crystals. "These are powerful ice crystals," she said. "Watch …"

Miss Linen tipped some of the crystals on to the cape. Soon it was covered with a sheet of ice. "I'm not cold!" said Jin.

Just then, there was a strange sucking noise.
The jar of ice crystals shot out of Miss Linen's hands towards the window in the roof.

"My ice crystals!" cried Miss Linen. "Someone's stealing them! We must get them back. The thief could use them to freeze the city!"

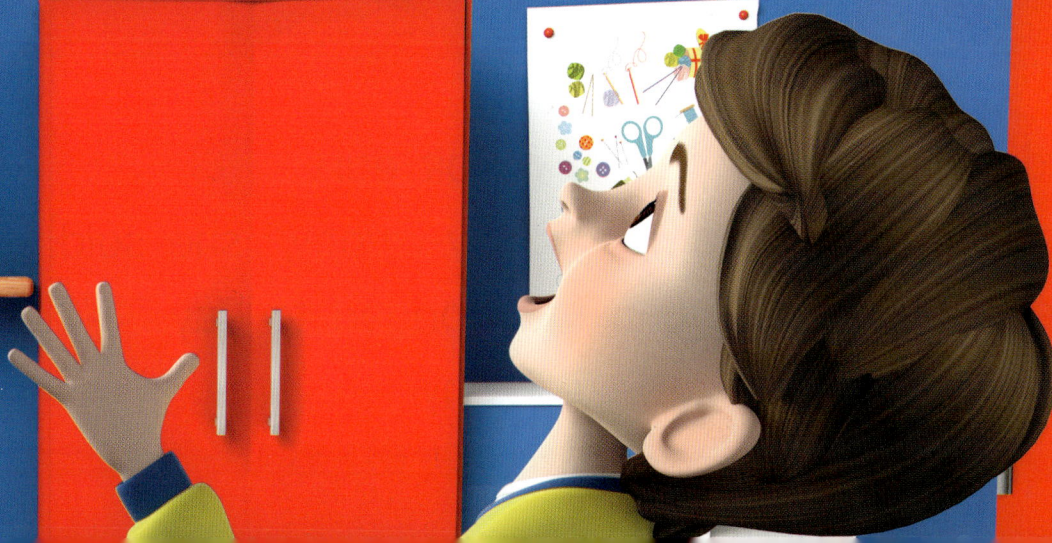

whooosh

Jin looked up to see a pair of rabbit ears.
Miss Linen frowned. "That's a bunny-wunny," she said.
Jin gasped. The bunny-wunnies belonged to Ray
Ranter, arch-enemy of Hero Academy.

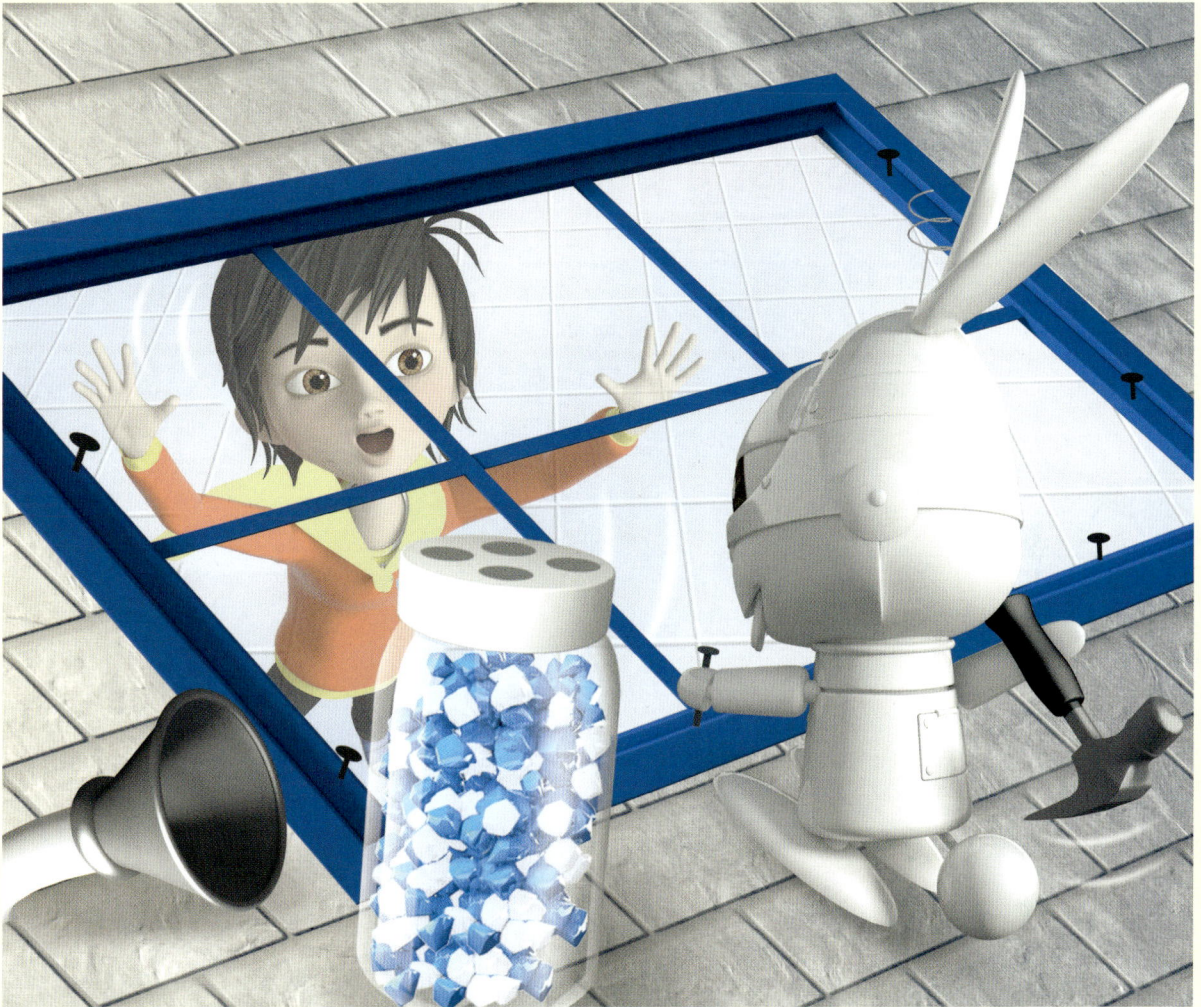

"Don't worry," said Jin. "I'll get the crystals back."
He took off, but the bunny-wunny slammed the
window and nailed it shut.
"I'll have to go the long way round," Jin said.
"I'll come with you," said Ben.

Jin and Ben ran out of the classroom. "Come on, Slink," said Jin, as they charged down the stairs. "We've got a bunny-wunny to catch!"

When they got outside, Ben said, "Do you think the bunny-wunny is still on the roof?"

"I don't know. I'll check," Jin replied. "But first …"

Jin, Ben and Slink spun into their superhero costumes.

Swoop

Combat Cat

Sprint

Swoop flew up. "No bunny-wunny here," he shouted.
Then he spotted something. "Wait! It's climbing down
the drainpipe!"

Swoop peered down at the bunny-wunny.
"It's heading for that van," he shouted. "Stop it!"

The bunny clung on to the back of the van.
Sprint shot after it.
Swoop and Combat Cat followed Sprint
out into the streets of Lexis City.

The heroes chased the van out of the city, over a bridge, to a huge metal shed.

"It's locked," said Sprint.

Ray Ranter was inside the shed, clutching the jar of ice crystals. He had a jetpack strapped to his back.

"You can't escape!" yelled Swoop.

"You're wrong about that!" Ranter replied.

Ranter switched on his jetpack and zoomed into the sky.

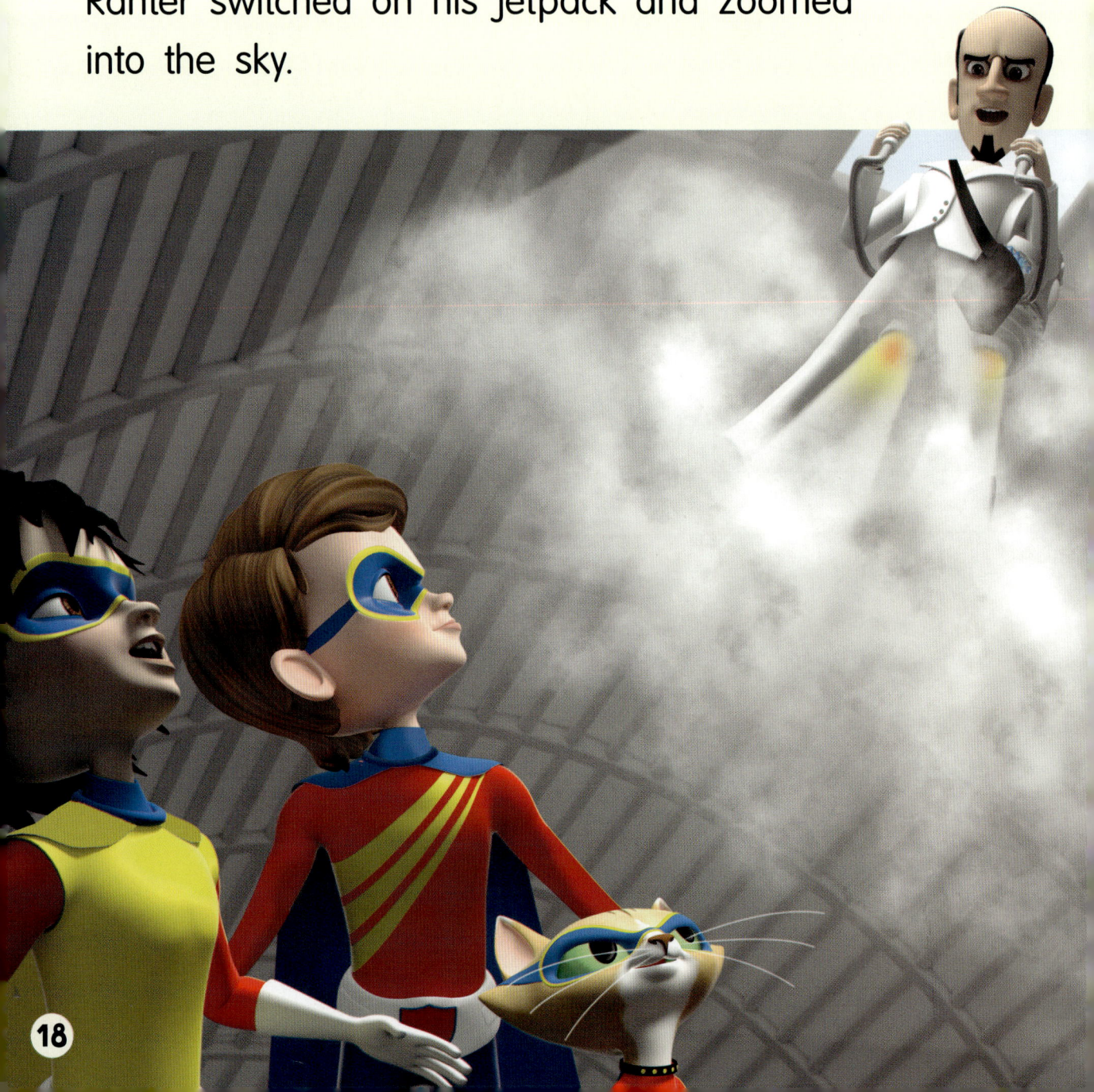

Ray Ranter flew up to a huge cloud. He sprinkled the ice crystals over it. A thick snowstorm began to fall. "I love snow," Ranter chuckled. "So white and clean!"

Swoop pulled Miss Linen's cape around himself. He flew up into the cloud.

When Ranter saw Swoop, he got a shock and dropped the jar of ice crystals.

"No!" Ranter yelled.

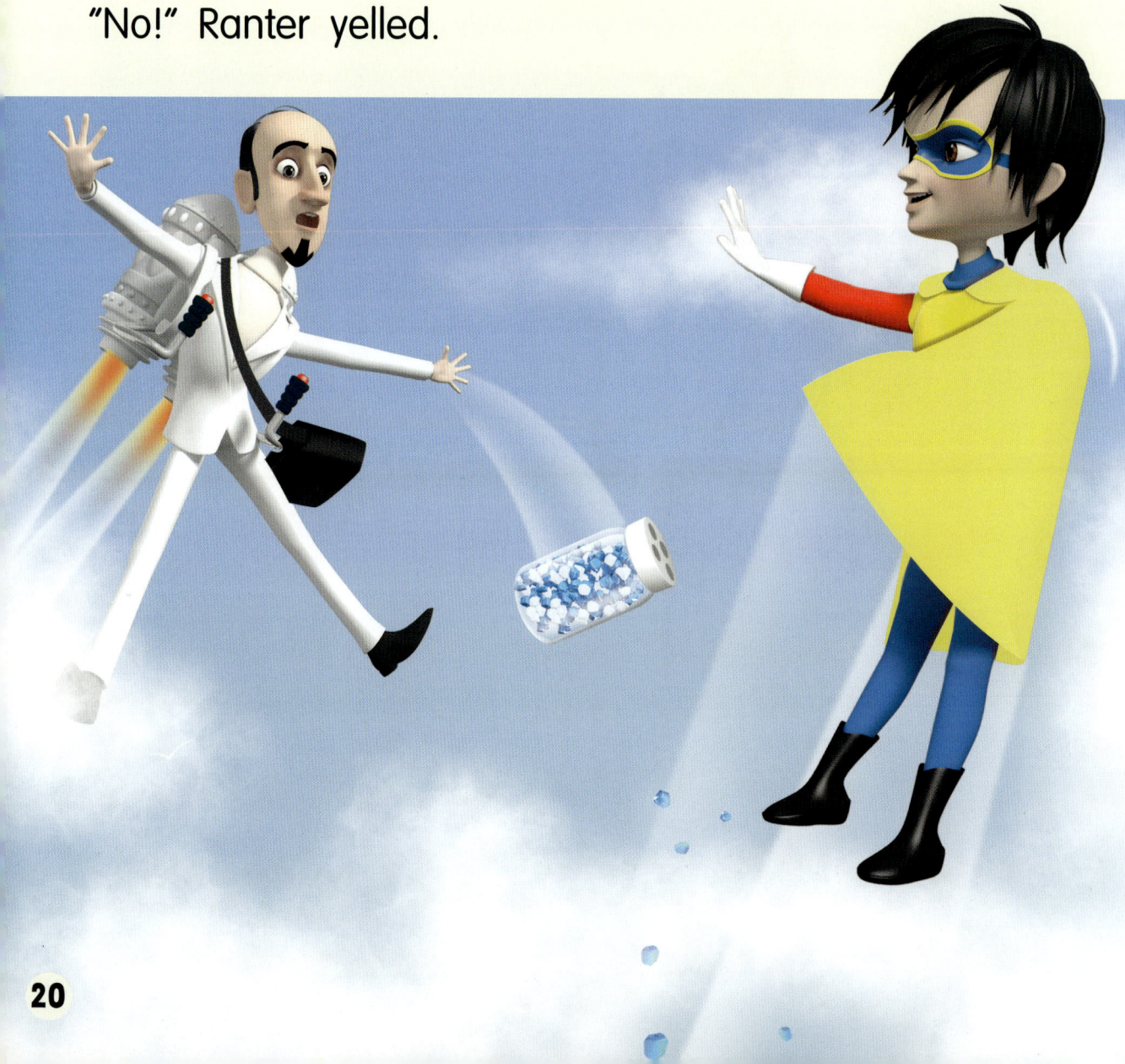

Swoop zoomed down. He managed to grab the jar just in time.

"Phew!" he said. "Now let's get these crystals back to school."

As Swoop, Sprint and Combat Cat hurried into school, some of the ice crystals spilled out. They made a sheet of ice.

Swoop, Sprint and Combat Cat slid along the ice and landed in a heap next to Miss Linen.

"My ice crystals!" she said. "Well done!"

Retell the story ...